Sheila's Guide to
Fast & Easy Kolkata/Calcutta

By

Sheila Simkin

1

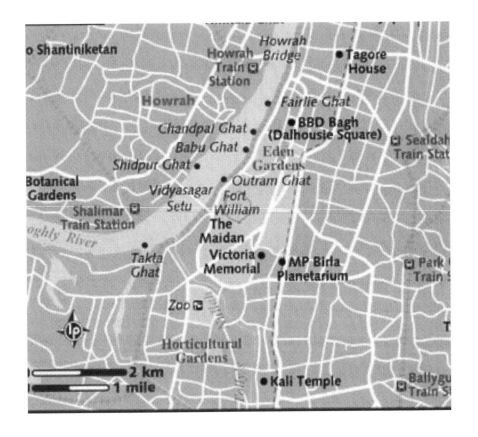

Sheila Simkin, a native Chicagoan, has been traveling the world since 1960. The travel bug first hit on her honeymoon in Miami. Fidel Castro had just taken over Cuba and lured by rock-bottom prices, Sheila sweet-talked her then husband into abandoning Miami for Cuba. That marked the beginning of her lifetime travel passion and addiction.

There are very few countries that are **not** on her to-see list no matter how remote and/or difficult they may be. The U.S. State Department recognizes 193 independent countries and she has visited 150 in over 40 years of travel (but...who's **counting**). Touring, hiking, trekking, rafting, snowshoeing, skiing, volunteering on archaeological digs, family trips and, she must admit, occasionally sitting on a beach or compulsively shopping.

Travels With Sheila.com attempts to deliver the hard facts. Answer questions that will help you plan your holiday. Whether it be a tight or upscale budget, Sheila has probably been there...done it. She has built up a network of trusted tour operators who will plan an individualized trip and arrange treks for around the same price a group tour would charge. Perhaps, even for **less**. Sheila will give information about pensions, inns, hotels, train travel, air, adventures without sugarcoating.

Sheila is **not** a Travel Agent, has no affiliation with any agency or airline and tells it as she sees it. Her goal is to encourage you to take the big step and travel to more exotic, remote destinations by providing tips, anecdotes and reassurance that, yes, you will come back alive. Visit: www.TravelsWithSheila.com and Happy traveling.

6

INTRODUCTION

Kolkata/Calcutta, and all of India, can be dirty, hot, congested, chaotic; has heart-wrenching poverty, some of the worst roads in the world, and demands patience along with constant vigilance regarding water and food but...Kolkata is one of my favorite cities despite all of this. **Don't think of Kolkata as -- "Mother Theresa = dying in streets."**

You may be surprised to learn that Kolkata is regarded as India's **intellectual and cultural** capital and has a profusion of colonial architecture! If you find **that** hard to believe, cheer on the horses at the venerable, veddy old, Royal Calcutta Turf Club, built in 1820; smell the roses in The Kolkata Wholesale Flower Market; explore the Kumartuli District where sculptors fashion gigantic effigies of gods; visit Hindu Temples, Churches and Synagogues; eat wonderful food; and while walking sandals into the ground, prepare to see even more! India is also one of the most **colorful and interesting countries in the world**. Prepare to **never** know what you are going to see on any given day.

If you want the most bang for your buck and see some of the most unusual sights in the world, **explore** Kolkata, India. **Are you ready?**

Sheila's Guide to Kolkata tells the good and the bad as **she** sees it. **Please visit Travels With Sheila Channel on YouTube.com to watch the videos.** On Sheila's last day in Kolkata, a man walked down Sudder Road (a busy, main street) with a **live sheep** slung over his back while his small son led their herd of goats down the middle of the road! If that doesn't stop you in your tracks, nothing will. Get ready to visit, and **enjoy**, Kolkata; brimming with impressive sights.

Sheila

PLANNING

When to Go

October to March is the perfect time with pleasant weather and festivities: Durga, Laxmi, and Diwali.

Air

International
Begin by flying into Netaji Subhash Bose International Airport (CCU), Kolkata's International Gateway; a shabby piece of work that should be replaced and had slow moving lines through immigration. Air India, British Airways, Lufthansa, Jet Airways, Thai Airways, Singapore Airlines, are just a few of the many airlines who fly to Kolkata. There are some great International and Domestic fares to India on the Internet. Visit the well-known websites: orbitz.com, kayak.com, cheapoair.com to see what works best for you.

> **TIP**: Save your hard-earned miles for First or Business Class on long-distance flights (the only way we can afford to fly in those sections) and economy on short-hauls. It may only be 20,000 miles for a short-haul ticket.

Domestic
Air routes connect Kolkata with at least 30 other cities in India.

No lollygagging is allowed when you fly India's domestic airlines. They load, check manifest and **leave** if everyone is on board. Sometimes, 10 minutes **ahead** of schedule. If you're not on board, you'll hear announcements until departure time. After that, tough luck.

Flying Internationally OUT of India
Pay attention to what time your outbound flight **leaves**. International Airlines usually leave Mumbai, Delhi, Kolkata at ungodly hours in the wee, small hours of the morning. For example, Lufthansa flies out of Mumbai back to Frankfurt at **3:25a**. **Even IF**, a big **if**, your India trip ends in one of those three cities, you still have decisions to make:

> Pay the hotel for a late check-out and stay in your room until midnight;

> Check out and wile away the time **somewhere**;

> Drive to the airport and attempt to enter. India airports usually **will not let you enter until three hours before flight time**. Airports have, what I refer to as, a "holding pens" outside the main terminals to sit in with toilet facilities, and food concessions; and/or

> Find a cheap hotel close to the airport that gives **free** transfers.

Decision-making never ends...

Transport To/From The Airport

Kolkata International Airport is located approximately 20 kilometers/11 miles from the city center. Ask for transport information while still inside the Arrival Hall to help make a decision.

Taxis
Taxis are the easiest way to travel into Kolkata center. Take a **prepaid** taxi, approximately 150-250 Rupees ($30-50 U.S.), depending on your final destination. An early in the morning, fly-by-night taxi will cost only $10-12 U.S., more about this in the Hotel Section.

Volvo Bus Service
These air conditioned buses have five different routes and are cheap (20-60 Rupees). Check to see if any of their routes pass close to your destination. If so, take a taxi from where the bus lets you off. If you are arriving in the early morning hours, **take the prepaid taxi**.

Hotel shuttles
Hotels can make prior arrangements.

Long Distance Buses and Trains

There are long distance buses and trains galore. The two major railway stations are Howrah and Sealdah. Check with a local travel agent for your best travel options. I recommend using a local agent to do the work. We changed reservations from train to air through our agent. They issued an e-ticket on Kingfisher Airlines, took credit card, sent "boy" to the train station to cancel reservation, and refunded $5 after cancellation fees. Worth every Rupee.

On the other hand, Justine, from New Zealand (whom we met in Sunderbans), was traveling around India using public transportation. She booked a rail ticket on-line and wanted to exchange it. Went to the RR station where personnel refused to exchange her ticket. Why? Since it was originally booked over the Internet, this ticket had to be **changed** on the Internet, even though there wasn't an **Internet** in that town. Since Justine was traveling that day, she had to buy a new ticket.

> **TIP**: Expect high frustration levels when **booking tickets** independently traveling through India. No worries if you are with a group or have a guide. Independent travelers should spend the few extra Rupees to let a local agent deal with the hassles. Case in point -- above.

Local Transportation in Kolkata

Rickshaw
Kolkata/Calcutta is one of the few cities in the world where drivers still pull their rickshaws by hand. My heart went out to these proud men trotting down the streets (usually bare foot) for pennies, dragging a heavy, tattered rickshaw behind them and not begging. Don't think this is for tourists because it's not. The locals use this form of transportation all the time with an average cost of 3-4 Rupees.

Taxi

There are over 70,000 metered taxis. Expect to be **overcharged**. There's no way around it unless a local is riding with you. After a screaming match with one driver, our guide told us that **meters aren't up-to-date**, and **double** the meter rate would be the correct amount. How would we know that? Now you know to **double** whatever the meter says!

> **TIP:** Always grab your hotel business card to find the way back or to tell cheap taxis **where** you are staying. It's very easy to get turned around in the maze of streets running on angles.

Tour Operators

Travels With Sheila current go-to-**India** tour operator is Footloose India (footlooseindia.com). They arrange **private, and custom tours**. For group travel contact, Adventure Center (adventurecenter.com) who represents: Exodus, Intrepid, Gecko, and Peregrine. Surf the Internet and you'll see there is no shortage of tour operators, and companies that have the perfect group for you, or who will arrange a vacation to your exact specifications.

Travels With Sheila does not get freebies or discounts for recommending Footloose or any other tour operator!

Hotel and guesthouses will be more than happy to assist you. Everyone has a "brother" who will be glad to take you..... (Fill in the blanks.) Make a **tentative plan of what to see**.

Hotels

Information is inside this Guide to Kolkata.

Restaurants and Food

Information is inside this Guide to Kolkata.

Currency

Indian Rupee (IDR) is the official currency and there is no problem exchanging GBP Sterling, Euros or U.S. Dollars in India. ATMs are easy to find at the airport and throughout Kolkata. When using ATM machines in India, **do the math before stepping into the booth and enter enough 00's**! For example: 49R=$1 US, 490R= $10, 4,900R=$100; 68R=1 Euro, 684R=10 Euros, 6485R=100 Euros.

> **TIP:** Use a money belt, leave good jewelry at home and exercise caution.

Visas

Visas are required for all visitors to India (except citizens of Nepal and Bhutan) and you **cannot get a Visa on Arrival.** We got smart a few years ago and got a 10-year Visa for not much more than a one-year Visa. Our thinking was even if it was only used twice during the next 10 years, we'd come out ahead, eliminating the hassle of getting a new one. Visitors staying in India for less than 72 hours can obtain a **Transit Visa**. Check with your nearest Indian Embassy for up-to-date Visa information. The latest kicker from the India Government is there must be a **two-month period between visits**. Keep that in mind.

Travel Insurance

Some don't buy travel insurance, we always do...just in case. Vacations are too costly to risk losing everything if any problems arise. Contact **Travel Guard** (travelguard.com) or **Travelex** (travelex.com) for insurance needs.

Health & Safety

I always check the **Centers for Disease Control** (cdc.gov) updates to see what they suggest. There is a risk of Malaria in India and Lariam (generic is Mefloquine) is the Malaria prophylaxis we use. A Tetanus booster is the most important inoculation in my estimation (we keep ours up-to-date religiously). It is not commonly known that you can get **Lockjaw** from contaminated dirt and even surface abrasions. Most people think that only a deep cut puts them at danger...not so. Hepatitis A and B are second on the list. Bring your other personal "drugs of choice."

> **TIP**: Antibiotics can be bought over-the-counter in India without a Doctor's prescription, but not "Controlled substances."

Even though bottled water is available throughout India, consider bringing iodine tablets for emergency purification situations. Don't even **think** of using tap water! **WASH YOUR HANDS...KEEP HANDS AWAY FROM EYES!** (ex-Marine, husband Steve, picked up a nasty eye infection in China). Otherwise, cleanliness is next to Godliness when traveling India.

Kolkata is currently safe to visit. Get up-to-date travel warnings from U.K. Foreign and Commonwealth Office (fco.gov.uk) and United States (travel.state.gov) websites.

Equipment

Cameras! Camcorder. Binoculars as well as a flashlight (torch) and Nalgene water bottles. Even a small keychain flashlight will come in handy; help you find the way from bed to bathroom, and is invaluable if electricity ever fails during the night. Don't forget disinfectant and a few small, plastic bags.

Clothing

It would be **hot and humid**. Most of India is hot and humid all year round. The winter dry season runs from October to March. A **hat**, capris or long pants, T-shirts and sandals for every day made it a very casual trip.

> **TIP**: Wear **sandals throughout India**. Shoes are not permitted in temples. Bring along a pair of "temple socks" if padding around barefoot bothers you. Socks **are** permitted;

What to See and Do in Kolkata

Information is inside this Guide to Kolkata.

Important Tips

⭐ Don't forget to call your ATM issuer and credit card companies, with international destination(s) information. Fraud, and identity theft, is at an all time high around the globe. You **don't** want the unpleasant surprise after handing over your credit card, or inserting your trusty ATM card in the machine, of seeing the nasty word "**DENIED**" pop up. It may not happen on your first transaction, but I'll bet a dozen doughnuts, it happens on the second. Make that telephone call to avoid embarrassment (and panic) upon hearing, "...so sorry, Madame, your card has been denied..."

⭐ Use an **ATM card for local currency** even if the bank tacks on a service charge. There are bancomats in 99% of the airports, railway stations, up and down streets, throughout the world.

⭐ **Do not,** under any circumstances, exchange money at home for your destination currency. The Euro is currently trading at 1.42 Euros to $1 U.S. In other words (because the Euro is confusing), it will cost you $1.42 U.S. to get 1 Euro. At almost all airport currency booths, it will cost you $1.62 to get 1 Euro, an additional 20 cents on each dollar. Additionally, do your very best to return home without any foreign currencies unless planning a return trip. Considering 2011 Currency Exchange Rates at O'Hare International Airport, you'll lose forty-two cents on every dollar. That's how banks and airport currency exchanges stay in business. Use those ATM cards!

⭐ Pack an **extra pair of glasses**. ex-Marine forgot his on the Annapurna Sanctuary Trek in Nepal. First, one earpiece broke off, followed by the other earpiece the next day. Unable to see without his glasses, we **DUCT-TAPED** the earpieces on each day.

⭐ **Don't** eat perishable **food** that's been sitting in the sun and/or outside all day. Food poisoning occurs in clean restaurants too, not just in India, but throughout the world. Idiotic Sheila got a wicked case of food poisoning **eating off a cruise ship buffet,** that had -- **food sitting in the sun**.

⭐ Don't pay more than 12 Rupees for a 1 liter bottle and you **do need water** unless you choose to drop Iodine tablets into the tap water. Even the locals drink bottled water if they can afford it.....

⭐ Make **copies of passport and visas**. Hotels request them when checking in and they must also be shown at security checkpoints.

⭐ Don't forget **earplugs**. Useful in even the best hotels as protection against very loud guests. I never leave home without them.

Welcome to Kolkata/Calcutta, India!

MORE IMPORTANT INFORMATION AND TRIVIA

India

No - India is not filled with people dying along the roads...filth and dirt everywhere (a question often asked of us). There is poverty. There are dirty areas. Don't we have the same? There is begging. More so around the famous tourist spots. Get a grip, folks and don't be frightened away by all those "stories";

If you are willing to stay in small but clean hotels or guesthouses, and eat in local restaurants, **India is a huge bargain.** A double room in most places including a bathroom with a Western toilet ranges about **$10-12 a NIGHT!** There is a reason why you see thousands of backpackers and others on a strict budget traveling in this country;

Prefer a **luxury hotel**? This is the place! Pay less than a comparable luxury hotel would be in Europe or the United States and the service will be so outstanding, you will be spoiled for life;

Antibiotics and drugs, other than controlled substances, are available over-the-counter in India. I checked prices on Generic Lariam (Malaria pills), 130 Rupees for (2) pills, around $3.00 U.S. That sounded terribly expensive to me until I returned home and discovered the lowest price through an online Canadian drug supplier was $44.51 U.S. for 8, over **$5.00 U.S. per pill**. Now I know, and you know to do your prescription shopping here;

Internet usually costs around 20R/hour. India cybercafes have a really neat security method. Show passport or identity card. Hold passport/card facing computer screen - click. Face built-in camera on screen - click. Fill in personal information. A one-time process as long as you **return** to the same internet office/cafe. If you go elsewhere, prepare to go through the entire process again. Wi-Fi is commonly available throughout India;

Take, and use, **a telephoto lens**, essential when you want to remain unobtrusive. That being said, Indian people not only love having their photograph taken, but are even happier to have their photograph taken with **you**. Pack extra batteries and memory cards;

Don't expect the same **climatic** conditions throughout India. India has deserts, glaciers, tropical regions, rain forests, islands; all have different **monsoon seasons**. I once scheduled a trek in the Himachal Pradesh, not realizing it was rainy season. Duh... Check the weather before you go.

Prepare to do **a slew** of tipping in India. They earn so little, how can you not tip? It wouldn't surprise me if tipping surpassed what we spent on **food**;

Kolkata/Calcutta

13

Kolkata/Calcutta is called "City of Joy" because the people are so easily pleased;

The Bathroom situation. Go into hotels or guesthouses while touring and **ask nicely**, to use their bathrooms. Once you leave your hotel, there **are** no more clean toilets;

The hand-pulled rickshaws can weigh more than 20 kilos/44 pounds (before adding the **rider(s)' weight**), and can only be found in **Central** Kolkata. Elsewhere, the rickshaws are pulled by bicycles or motorbikes. Kolkata/Calcutta is one of the few cities in the world where drivers still pull their rickshaws by hand. Don't think this is for tourists because it's not. The locals use this form of transportation all the time with an average cost of 3-4 Rupees;

Kolkata is the only Indian City that still operates **trams**, once pulled by horses;

Bengalis are considered to be extremely **loud**, even by other Bengalis. Ordinary conversations sound like heated arguments;

The Kolkata population exceeds **13 million people**. More than **one million** people make their way into the city each day for work;

Calcutta (British name) was the capital of India during the British Raj until 1911, and British Raj buildings still remain. Some are hollow shells; others are being rebuilt; and still more are in use, despite their dilapidated condition; and

Yes, "**Calcutta**" was changed to "**Kolkata**" in January 2001, with many conflicting explanations given to why it was changed.

Again, we think India is one of the world's best-kept secrets with gracious, friendly people, and you are almost guaranteed to see something unique, or different, daily.

HOTELS

We arrived at Kolkata International Airport in the early morning with reservations at Lytton Hotel (lyttonhotelindia.com). There was **no** ATM machine outside customs and Information told us to walk one-block over to the Domestic Terminal to find one. Following their recommendation, we got to the ATM with a big sign, "Out of Order." (Taxis will accept Dollars and Euros if necessary.)

Using A Gypsy Taxi

All taxis in front of International Arrivals had left by now with only one fly-by-night taxi remaining. He began negotiating, quoted a $10 U.S. rate to Lytton Hotel (showed us a rate card), and we jumped in. Pulling away, the driver changed his mind and said the fare would be $12, not $10. **No!** We've been there, done it, and told him to let us out of the cab **NOW!** Resolve written over every pore of our bodies, he capitulated, went back to the original $10 and drove off into the darkness.

The next 30-45 minutes was a terrifying ride down streets lined with shanties, parked buses and trucks; dirty streets filled with garbage, he ran red lights, and bumped over trolley lines. Steve and I gave each other a glance now and then; both thinking that it was just a matter of minutes before we were robbed and killed. Would anyone ever find our dead bodies? Eventually, the gypsy taxi turned down one last street with people sleeping in the bushes and pulled up to a gate that had **Lytton Hotel** written on the outside wall. The omnipresent security guard (every restaurant, shop and hotel has a security man posted in front) looked in the taxi, saw two western faces and let the taxi in. A frightening ride, but it demonstrated that not everyone in Kolkata was out to rob you blind.

Lytton Hotel, Kolkata

My heart fell, and I was already wondering what kind of minimal hotel this was. In the darkness, our first impression of the budget to moderate Lytton Hotel was **underwhelming,** especially with people sleeping in **bushes** outside. The porter escorted us to a dated room with bathroom, and a room boy came in to make up the bed. Dead on our feet by now, neither of us cared if this was a **hovel** as long as it had a **bed**. Perhaps the Lytton Hotel would look better after some sleep.

Good news, the three-star Lytton Hotel looked **much** nicer in the daylight, and was ideally located in the Chowringhee area on Sudder Street, a longtime favorite of budget travelers and **safe**. Other in-the-know Westerners (primarily French people) were staying here beside us. The Chowringhee area is close to all the action, and only a stone's throw to The Maidan, shops and restaurants. The very popular Lytton Hotel has: 79 rooms, free Wi-Fi in public areas, restaurant, coffee shop, airport transport, and buffet breakfast, included in the rates. Minimum rates are approximately $100 U.S. for a double room.

The delicious International breakfast buffet served different choices each day. Indian food; yogurt; juice; eggs made to order; the ubiquitous British favorite, baked beans; and unexpected "breakfast foods" like **vegetable tetrazzini**.

Happy now, our spirits rose even higher when we discovered the famous **five-star** Oberoi-Grand Kolkata, (oberoikolkata.com) was only a three blocks away.

The entire area around Sudder Street is saturated with hotels and guesthouses. I suggest surfing over to: hotels.com, booking.com, and asia.com, just to mention a few to choose from hundreds of hotels and guesthouses in Kolkata; ranging in price from $13 U.S. for a one-star hotel up to megabucks at the Park, Oberoi and Taj Hotels.

RESTAURANTS AND FOOD

You will not starve in India. Food is extremely cheap and **Indian food** is **delicious**. It does **not** exclusively consist of curry. (The first thing our friends always comment on is: "Don't you get tired of eating curry all the time?") We've discovered a wide-range of breads, vegetables and Tandoori (our favorite) over time. India has a bountiful array of cuisines throughout the country. And yes, we **have** also eaten curry. Dine like a king/queen in local restaurants with excellent food for perhaps $1.00 U.S. maximum.

If you don't like Indian food, there are continental restaurants; most places (including little hole in the wall Indian restaurants) serve American-style breakfasts, and there is always Pizza Hut, KFC and McDonald's.

Lytton Hotel served meals throughout the day and, jet lagged, we usually tucked into either a late lunch or early dinner, ordering our favorite Indian foods: Rice Biryani, Tandoori Chicken and *Naan* Bread.

Rice *Biryani* - Bhasmati rice with meat, fish, eggs or vegetables;

Tandoori* Chicken** - Roasted chicken, marinated in yogurt and spices, cooked in a ***Tandoor Oven. ***Tandoor*** ovens aren't usually turned on until evening in India. Ask, if the oven is on **before** ordering to avoid being disappointed; and

Naan, a leavened, oven-baked flatbread.

We ate delicious Chinese food one night at Tung Fong Restaurant, 225B Park Street, walking distance from the hotel. Large quantities of food cost $10 U.S. for the two of us. Back home in the good old U.S. of A., it would have been a minimum of $35.

The Bengalis are great food lovers, take pride in their cuisine and eat fish daily. I am extremely leery over eating fish in hot climates thanks to quite a few episodes of food poisoning. You never know how long the fish sat in the sun before being sold to restaurants, and then, how it was refrigerated. We had absolutely no problem with food or water. Use **common sense**. Drink **bottled water only**, don't eat raw foods, "cook, peel or forget it..."

Find an Internet **Indian Food Glossary**, print it off, and bring with. Do as I say, not as I did, and you'll avoid an unexpected entree on your plate. *Seekh Kebab* is **not** "Shish Kebob." *Seekh Kebab* is made of minced meat with spices, grilled, and served on skewers. Delicious, but not what we thought it was. A few other typical foods to know about are:

Kati Kebob Rolls. Pieces of spicy chicken are wrapped in *Paratha* (another Indian flat bread) that has been coated with egg;

Mughali Paratha. A *Paratha* stuffed with minced meat);

Sweets. Bengalis love sweets, as do I. Once we discovered David Nahoum's famous Nahoum's Confectioners shop in the New Market right behind Lytton Hotel, we bought and tried different goodies from him. Ask for directions inside the New Market; and

It is important to know that throughout India, **Coffee and/or tea** is usually served with **spoonfuls** of sugar pre-added. **Ask before you order**!

BEGGERS AND TOUTS

Learn to ignore the beggers and touts, usually found where tourists gather. Don't answer...acknowledge...or try to be polite. Put blinders on or you'll **hate** Kolkata. I absolutely detested the tiny, skinny woman beggars around New Market who would sneak up behind me, and begin jabbing a finger like **steel** into my bicep, continuously. It was only when I finally got smart and had Steve stand between us, they would stop. They don't touch men, only women.

Don't give anything to beggars! Whether they are children or adults. Neither pens, money, nor sweets. Handouts set a precedent for those tourists who follow, and cacophonies of "pen, pen, pen" reverberates from the smallest hamlet to the biggest city. Bring goods with you to leave at a school, hospital or charity in India; they'll be happy to accept. And whatever you may give is never enough. Case in point -- At an airport, a man literally **yanked** the suitcases out of ex-Marine's hand, and walked into the parking lot with us running after him. Jet-lagged, Steve gave him a tip even though he hadn't done anything. The man looked at the money, and said, "Is that all you're giving me?" I angrily shouted back, "Then give it back, if it's not enough!" He, and the tip, disappeared.

If you've seen *Slum Dog Millionaire*, do you remember the scene where *Latika* was forced to take a crying baby to beg with? The most upsetting incident out of 10 trips to India happened while sitting in our vehicle with guide and driver in Kolkata. Stopped at a red light in traffic, a begger boy, perhaps 9-10 years old stood in the middle of traffic, carrying a 4-5 month old half-naked, crying baby under one arm. He walked up to our rolled up car windows and **banged** (not tapped but **banged**) the baby's head **against** the window to get money. Of course, the baby cried louder, and when we didn't respond, he continued banging the baby's head against the window, repeatedly. When I looked the other way, he walked around the car to Steve's side and began hitting the baby's head against **his** window before moving off to another car to repeat. If that doesn't make you ill, nothing will.

Our guide and driver ignored this because it happens all the time. Whose baby is it? Where does the baby comes from? Nobody knows. These poor babies become brain-damaged and are disposable "things" for the beggars to use and discard when the baby dies. You **can't** give money because it just encourages the beggar to keep going from car to car. To be perfectly fair, this was a first. Beggers, yes. Touts, plentiful but never deliberate cruelty. Despite the poverty, we never felt **threatened or unsafe** walking the vibrant Kolkata streets. In fact, the Bengalis are known for friendliness and warm welcomes.

WHAT TO SEE AND DO IN KOLKATA

New Market

Outside Lytton Hotel, it was make a left, make another left at the first block and go straight one block for one block more. The New Market will be right in front of you. There is an ATM across from the New Market and it was time to withdraw money. Rupees were converting at: 49 Rupees=$1 U.S. during this visit (we rounded to 50). In a jet lag fog, we eliminated a "0" the first time and entered 1,500 Rupees. Thirty Dollars U.S. chugged out of the machine.

Totally confused, we did a **big "no-no"** and let a local into the ATM booth with us who offered to help when we explained the situation. Our faith in humankind was restored. He helped us enter **15,000 Rupees = $300.00 U.S.** That was more like it and ended up being more than enough money for three weeks in India.

> **TIP:** Make sure you enter enough **000's** to get the right amount of money.

New Market is technically located on Lindsay Street, off Chowringhee Road. Besides the 2,000 stalls inside grouped according to the type of goods they sell, the entire perimeter is lined with people selling a variety of goods. This market is the oldest, and best known market in Kolkata, built by the British in 1874. Named after Sir Stuart Hogg, Commissioner then, the square in front of New Market has an impressive colonial clock tower. **New Market is closed on Sunday.** You will be approached in the square by "touts" aka "guides," eager to "escort" you to shops that will pay them a commission. It's not a bad idea to hire one. The lanes inside New Market lead on angles in different directions. Just keep a firm hand, agree on a guiding price and don't let yourself get suckered into buying something at an overinflated price. **Bargain hard!**

Nahoum's Confectioners shop is located in the approximate center, but we still got completely lost in the maze of lanes and had to ask for directions. Backpacks filled with cupcakes and wonderful buns, we then loaded up on liter bottles of water (*Pani*) before heading back to the Lytton Hotel. We'd revisit the New Market another day. Don't pay more than 12 Rupees for a 1 liter bottle and you'll need quantities of water in Kolkata's heat and humidity.

Chowringhee Road Area

The best way of seeing Kolkata is by walking. This is the only way to **really** get a feel for Kolkata; not by "sightseeing" but immersing yourself into the chaos. Directions from hotel staff, it was gird loins and head outside on Sudder Street. Little yellow Ambassador taxis, and barefoot, painfully thin (but strong) rickshaw pullers waited around for a fare; a few beggars and homeless people, slept in the bushes, and doorways while others washed themselves in running water. One of the many Mother Theresa Homes for the Dying and Indigent wasn't far away, and a building across the street distributed free food to the poor several times a week. Even so, you'll see these sights all over Kolkata/Calcutta. No one will bother you!

Continue walking west on Sudder Street for a few blocks. dead-ending at Chowringhee Road, running north and south. The Indian Museum will be on your left, the green Maidan, directly in front of you. The **Maidan** is the largest urban park in Kolkata. It's 3 km/1.8 mile field includes: the city's famous cricket field; several football stadiums; Kolkata Race Course; and the Victoria Memorial.

Make a right on Chowringhee Road and begin walking north past the Oberoi as far as you can before feet give out. You'll pass: shops, restaurants, a million stalls, British Raj Landmark buildings, 18th- and 19th-century mansions. Many of these old houses were "landlord houses" built by merchants who received a portion of land to manage, and collect taxes, for the British. Landlords were allowed to keep 50 percent for themselves and, in the process, became quite rich and built their **own** grandiose houses. Anything with Landmark Status in Kolkata cannot be destroyed.

Old mansions are unexpectedly tucked into every quarter; Police officers, nattily dressed in whites, made valiant attempts to direct traffic; small trucks carried top-heavy loads; and twisted masses of electrical/telephone lines looped on posts. When you can no longer take another step, hail a taxi.

The Kolkata Wholesale Flower Market

Down by the Hooghly River and almost under the Howrah Bridge is the Kolkata Flower Market, open 24 hours a day and crammed to the brim with sellers and buyers. Before taking a deep breath and plunging into the chaos of the Flower Market, our guide Malini took us down steps onto the banks of the Hooghly River first; entering through dilapidated and crumbling buildings. We stood for a while watching the locals go about their early morning chores in this very polluted river. Polluted or not, a person has to use whatever is available to wash clothes and themselves.

The **Kolkata Wholesale Flower Market** is one of the Kolkata highlights. I dearly love flowers and the sight (and smell) of thousands of roses will forever remain with me. You can buy one dozen long stem red roses for less than $1.00 U.S. **That** blew my mind. The market is almost directly under the Howrah Bridge, itself a landmark. At one time, the Howrah Bridge was the **only** way across the Houghly River and is similar in size to Sydney Harbour Bridge in Australia. It is considered the **busiest bridge in the world** and everything from pedestrians...to bullock carts...to push carts...to automobiles...to bicycles, cross every day.

> TIP: Buyers and sellers **run** through the narrow lanes with humungous loads on their **heads**. Watch every **footstep**, where you **walk**, what's coming at you, and don't step in piles of **animal and human excrement!**

This 125-year flower market was gutted by a devastating fire in 2008 and rebuilt. The Kolkata Flower Market is eastern India's largest flower market with hundreds of stalls and people. One guesstimate? Approximately 2,000 flower growers from the surrounding areas come daily to sell; during wedding seasons and festivals, probably **double** that number.

There were garlands of Marigolds in bright yellow and orange -- carried on arms, heads -- piled into heaps on the ground. Women sat stringing Marigold garlands; used in Hindu festivals, to decorate the gods, and placed around visitors' necks in India. The colors were brilliant but I've never been a fan of the Marigold odor. People were selling, unloading trucks, unpacking a gazillion bags and boxes of flowers. A porter trotted by with **dozens of red roses on his head** while I stood entranced, inhaling the scent of roses permeating the air. I probably could have stood in raptures for ages but Malini said there was a lot to still see and do.

Put this excursion on your to-do list in Kolkata whether **you** love flowers. It was unforgettable.

Kolkata Clay Modelers

Leaving the Kolkata Flower Market, men were loading and unloading trucks filled with heavy bags of rice and grains. Sellers sold fruit and green coconuts to drink. Small carts carried cardboard. Locals picked through the garbage (remember *Slum Dog Millionaire?*). There was no end to the sights in Kolkata.

A short car ride to Kumartula, one of the oldest residential areas in Kolkata, with a high concentration of clay modelers, known as "Kumar." This district is kept busy throughout the year making icons of Hindu Gods and Goddesses, and wedding decorations. Diwali (the festival of lights) was over and since Holi (the festival of colors and spring) had not begun, most of the clay modelers weren't working today. A few were preparing deities made of bamboo, straw and clay, which are then decorated with color and cloth, but not many.

Queen Victoria Memorial

Before heading to the Queen Victoria Memorial and temples, we popped into the New Market for a few minutes to buy some buns (sweet rolls) at Nahum & Sons Confectionary (we were all starving) and the Oberoi to use a clean toilet.

> **TIP:** Look for a decent hotel and/or restaurant. Once you leave your hotel, **there are no clean toilets.**

The three of us snarfed down buns in the car and headed from north to south past the Maidan (a wide expanse of green) to the Victoria Memorial.

The Victoria Memorial was built in Italian Renaissance style by the British who tried to emulate the Taj Mahal, and contains a supposedly fantastic collection of memorabilia from Colonial days. Steve and I will have to believe Malani since we were just too tired to tour the inside. We contented ourselves with a walk across the Queen Victoria Memorial Bridge to look at the wonderful murals on the outside, paid our respects to the statue of Queen Victoria, and sat watching local tourists take in the memorial. The cover of this guide is of the Queen Victoria Memorial as seen from the Royal Calcutta Turf Club.

Dakshineshwar Temple

The Dakshineshwar Kali Temple is located across the Hooghly River in the north Kolkata area. Off with the shoes, paid a few Rupees to have them **watched** (they **would not** be there when leaving if you didn't), before heading inside. On weekends (which this was), there is a very long wait to enter the most important, nine-spired main temple in the center where Rama-krishna was a priest and reached his spiritual vision of the unity of all religions. The Dakshineshwar Temple was built in 1847 or 1855, depending who gives you the information, and is surrounded by 12 other temples dedicated to Shiva. Malini had two interesting "facts": If a worshipper visits and prays at all the temples in this complex, all sins are washed away; and the worship of "woman power" only takes place in the Bengali area.

Instead of standing in the very long line for the main temple, we walked out the courtyard to the Hooghly River and spent time watching the locals bathe before leaving the complex; every woman entering Dakshineshwar Kali Temple carried red flowers for offerings to Kali. "Red" is Kali's favorite color and she is considered the kindest and most loving of all the Hindu Goddesses.

Kalighat Temple

From Dakshineshwar Kali Temples, it was back to south Kolkata (not far from the Taj Bengal Hotel) where Kalighat (Kali) Temple is located. This temple was rebuilt in 1809 on the site of a much older temple. According to legend, when Parvati's corpse was cut up, one of her fingers (or toes) fell here. Thousands of pilgrims come daily to this temple, bringing Kali their problems and prayers for prosperity; returning when their prayers are fulfilled to express their gratitude.

We weren't allowed to enter the temple itself but Malini spoke to a store owner outside the Kalighat Temple who unlocked one door to a viewing area where we could see the Temple dome, and pool. Goddess Kali, receives a ceremonial bath every year by the head priest, and a man was busy cleaning out this fetid, slimy pool in preparation for the ceremony.

Kali also shows a destructive side and demands daily sacrifices. To accommodate this need, goats have their throats slit every morning and the meat is given to the poor during the day. We happily missed this. Watching all those water buffalo funeral sacrifices in Sulawesi was more than enough to satisfy my blood lust.

Mother Teresa's Hospital for the Dying Destitute is next door to the temple. Some people like to volunteer here and in some of other charities to teach, help bathe lepers, etc. Footloose Tours had asked if we were interested in assisting, and got a big, resounding **no** in return. Those wonderful volunteers are made of sterner stuff than we are.

The Royal Calcutta Turf Club

And now for something completely different! With a free day in Kolkata, Footloose Travel had suggested spending time at the venerable Royal Calcutta Turf Club (race course), built in 1820, **IF** the horses were running that day. It's difficult to get information on-line but the daily newspaper said races were scheduled. Good deal...*here they come spinning around the turn...*

Malini had pointed out the Royal Calcutta Turf Club to us yesterday (they have not changed the spelling of Calcutta to Kolkata), and we set out to walk there, calculating it was perhaps a 2-3 mile walk tops from Lytton Hotel. Off we went, a straight south shot down Chowringhee Road, past the green expanse of the Maidan with its park and cricket grounds (people exercise here in the morning); managed to cross the roads without getting run over, all the while inhaling tons of dust and pollution. The constant din of traffic, honking, buses spewing exhaust and heat was tiring but **finally** the Royal Calcutta Turf Club was in front of us.

A Day at The Horse Races
There is a 10 Rupee General Admission. Once inside the big, circular enclosure outside the grandstands, English-style bookmakers stand, writing the latest odds on slate boards, and taking bets. They don't take bets for less than 100 Rupees. We pondered, not nothing a thing about any of the horses running. Steve liked one horse, I liked "Rockstar" and bet 120 Rupees on Rockstar in the First Race. How were we to know there were parimutuel windows a little further on that took a bet for **10 Rupees**? Darn and Rats! With 49 Rupees to $1 U.S., I could have wagered like crazy.

My late father used to take his three little girls to the Race Track and I have fond memories of sitting in the stands, cheering on his bets, and eating junk food sold by every vendor that walked by.

Grateful and happy to sit in the grandstand with locals, we were completely unaware that the race was almost over until horses flew by us. The starting gate was on the far side of the track and we were looking in the wrong direction! Rockstar lost but we had such a good time. I had forgotten about the colorful jockey silks, how small the jockeys are, the magnificent gorgeous race horses, and general camaraderie. The Calcutta Turf Club had an added bonus of the Victoria Memorial in the distance.

Bagpipers play between races; women dressed in saris walked around the track after each race replacing the turf kicked up by the horses; locals kept coming up to talk to us, interested in the only westerners sitting in the general stands; and the race track was a blessed respite from the constant horn-blowing of traffic.

Three races later, we walked into the "Member's Only"/V.I.P. section for one last race (we must have looked "classier" than I thought) before leaving, and jumping into a cab back to the hotel. It was too darn hot to walk back.

Kolkata's Jewish Synagogues

Kolkata has always had a diverse community that includes: Chinese, Tamil, Armenian, Tibetan, Greek and Jews; India (historically) has provided shelter and asylum to people facing persecution. If someone doesn't take you by the hand and **show** you where the two synagogues *(..."synagogue" means house of assembly, house of worship...)* of Kolkata are, you'll **never** find the them. Both Magen David and Beth El Synagogues (Historic Protected Heritage Monuments) are buried in the extremely busy BBD Bagh (Dalhousie Square) area; the center of British power during the 1800's and reasonably close to the Kolkata Flower Market and Howrah Bridge. Down narrow streets, surrounded by busy wholesale/retail shops and warehouses, you not only will have trouble finding them but also need **written permission** to visit.

Malini tried to locate the synagogues during the Kolkata sightseeing tour without any success. At the end of our Orissa tour, we arrived back in Kolkata for a short day, and decided to revisit Nahoum's Confectioners shop in the New Market. Both to tell Mr. Nahum how disappointed we were over not finding the synagogues, and buy more delicious buns. Nahoum's was founded in 1902 and the original owner's grandson is the person you see for written permission.

Mr. Nahum instantly delegated one of his employees to jump in a taxi with us (Ha! For once the taxi driver couldn't charge us triple with a local along), take us to the first synagogue and give instructions to the caretaker there to walk us to the second synagogue where we'd find a taxi back to the New Market; extremely kind of him. The majority of Kolkata/Calcutta Sephardic Jews immigrated from Iraq and the Jewish community (approximately 6,000) has dwindled to only about 15 in Kolkata (per Mr. Nahum). The first recorded Jewish immigrant to Kolkata came from Syria in 1798.

Magen David Synagogue
You enter Magen David from a courtyard set back off Canning Street. It is the "newer" (built between 1883-1884), larger, and more ornate of the two synagogues. The Magen David Synagogue was founded by the Ezra family in memory of his father and is of post-Renaissance period design. The Ezra family was the most influential family in Kolkata at this time, and was also responsible for building Beth El Synagogue, the Chowringhee Mansions and Esplanade Mansions.

Similar to typical synagogues of this time, women would sit and worship separate from the men on the upper level gallery. Magen David Synagogue is the largest synagogue in the East, lit by gas, had beautiful stained glass windows and was ornately decorated. From Magen David Synagogue, the caretaker walked us 10 minutes away to Beth El Synagogue on Pollock Street.

Beth El Synagogue

Beth El Synagogue, constructed in 1856, had an outside *matzo* oven (unleavened bread) used for baking Passover *matzo* and *mikvah*, "*...a ritual purification and cleansing bath that Orthodox Jews take on certain occasions (as before Sabbath or after menstruation)...*" Beth El was smaller, older and more intimate that Magen David Synagogue. It was interesting to read the plaque outside stating the Ezra family bought the property and founded Beth El Synagogue with their own money. The plaque was erected by the congregation in gratitude and memory.

Steve and I were glad we made the effort to visit some of Kolkata's remaining Jewish history and, on a side note, the cab driver **tripled** the fare back to New Market....

THE FAMOUS AND "HOLY COWS" OF INDIA

"**Holy Cow**"... No, Chicago residents, Harry Caray did **not** coin that phrase. A first trip to India always astounds visitors. **Why** are all those cows sitting placidly in the middle of traffic? **Why** do people let them casually walk into their houses? **Why** are they everywhere you are? **Why** aren't these bony-looking bovines on farms where they belong? **What the heck is going on?**

Animal life is a central theme in Hindu life and in India - all animals are sacred. Even Jain nuns carried little mops to dust off the ground before siting to keep from crushing an insect!

Some trace the cow's sacred status back to Lord Krishna, one of Vishnu's eight incarnations. He is said to have appeared 5,000 years ago as a cowherd, and often described as *bala-gopala*, "The child who protects the cows." Another reason the cow is sacred to Hindus is the belief they can only reach heaven by crossing a mythological river holding the tail of a cow. Other scriptures identify the cow as the "mother" of all civilization, its milk nurturing the population. However, It's a different situation when the cows no longer produce milk. They are then abandoned on the road because it is **bad luck if a cow dies on your property**.

The cows that you see along the roads are usually the abandoned ones who create dangerous and massive traffic jams. It is astonishing that in 20+ years of travel through India, we've **never** seen any cow/motorized vehicle accidents. A citizen can even be sent to jail for killing or injuring a cow. Delhi is now experimenting with personnel who catch, and ship, the wayward cows outside the city limits to special reserves. Have you heard it all, now? Instead of wild game reserves, wild cow reserves?

When a cow dies a natural (or unnatural) death, it is skinned and then **buried**. They used to leave cows for the vultures but vultures are in scant supply because DDT killed them. Cows ate plants sprayed with DDT. DDT didn't harm the cows. When Cows died, vultures feasted on cows and the DDT in cow's bodies killed off the vultures. End of story...

To answer the question, "**Why** are all those cows sitting in the middle of traffic" - According to authorities, the exhaust, noise, etc., not only keeps flies off the cows but as an added bonus, the **exhaust fumes get them high**.

"Holy Cow!...I'm out of here...

29

HINDSIGHT IS 20/20

At **least** one more day spent in Kolkata would have given us time to:

Stroll around **BBD Bagh (Dalhousie Square)**, jam-packed with stores, stalls, warehouses and old colonial buildings; and

Revisit the **Victoria Memorial** to go **inside** and learn more about Kolkata's old colonial history.

How stupid not to exchange money **inside** the International Arrival Area at Kolkata Airport instead of looking for that nonfunctioning ATM. So what if we lost Rupees on the conversion? Penny wise and Pound foolish;

Always **count your money** before walking away from an currency exchange; even if there is a long line of people behind you. The employees consistently make "**mistakes**" (according to them when a recount showed the wrong amount); and

Make arrangements for a **pre-paid taxi** to your hotel from the Airport!

Kolkata can be humbling, and it definitely takes a go-with-the flow mentality to survive, but you won't regret the time and effort spent visiting and enjoying Incredible India!

Other Travel Guides by Sheila Simkin:

Sheila's 25 Best China Travel Tips
Sheila's 25 Best India Travel Tips
Sheila's 25 Best International Layover Hotels

Sheila's Guide to Albania
Sheila's Guide to Cairo
Sheila's Guide to Egypt Desert Travel
Sheila's Guide to European Train Travel

Sheila's Guide to Guizhou, China

Sheila's Guide to Gujarat, India
Sheila's Guide to Ladakh, India
Sheila's Guide to Orissa, India
Sheila's Guide to Zanskar, Ladakh, India

Sheila's Guide to Lesser Sundra Islands, Indonesia (Lombok, Sumbawa, Komodo, Rinca, Flores)
Sheila's Guide to Sulawesi, Indonesia

Sheila's Guide to Myanmar/Burma

Sheila's Guide to North Ethiopia
Sheila's Guide to Tribal South Ethiopia
Sheila's Guide to Unknown Ethiopia
Sheila's Guide to River Kwai Area, Thailand

Sheila's Guide to Fast & Easy Antalya
Sheila's Guide to Fast & Easy Bali, Indonesia
Sheila's Guide to Fast & Easy Bangkok
Sheila's Guide to Fast & Easy Beijing
Sheila's Guide to Fast & Easy Buenos Aires
Sheila's Guide to Fast & Easy Chiang Mai
Sheila's Guide to Fast & Easy Hanoi
Sheila's Guide to Fast & Easy Istanbul
Sheila's Guide to Fast & Easy Java, Indonesia
Sheila's Guide to Fast & Easy Manila
Sheila's Guide to Fast & Easy Nile Cruises
Sheila's Guide to Fast & Easy Shanghai
Sheila's Guide to Fast & Easy Singapore

Discover Ancient Thai Kingdoms: AYUTTHAYA, SUKHOTHAI AND LAMPANG

21993041R00017

Made in the USA
Columbia, SC
23 July 2018